**Bush
Theatre**

G000141313

Going Through

by Estelle Savasta
translated by Kirsten Hazel Smith

28 March – 27 April 2019
Bush Theatre, London

b.

Cast

Youmna	**Nadia Nadarajah**
Nour	**Charmaine Wombwell**

Creative Team

Playwright	**Estelle Savasta**
Translator	**Kirsten Hazel Smith**
Director	**Omar Elerian**
Associate Director	**Louise Stern**
Designer	**Rajha Shakiry**
Video Designer	**Nina Dunn**
Lighting Designer	**Josh Pharo**
Sound Designer	**Elena Peña**
Video Design Assistant	**Laura Salmi**
Costume Supervisor	**Alex Horner**
Assistant Director	**Emily Aboud**
Production Manager	**Phil Buckley**
Stage Manager	**Patricia Davenport**
Assistant Stage Manager	**Jacob Amos**

Cast

Nadia Nadarajah

Nadia trained at International Visual Theatre (Paris). Her theatre credits include: *A Christmas Carol* (Bristol Old Vic); *Hamlet* & *As You Like It* (Shakespeare's Globe); *The Unheard World* (Arlington Artist Centre, Newbury); *Our Town* (Royal Exchange, Manchester); *Untouchable* (RADA Festival); *The House of Bernarda Alba* (Royal Exchange, Manchester); *Can I Start Again Please* (UK Tour); *Notre Dame* (National Theatre); *Grounded* (Deafinitely Theatre at Park Theatre); *A Midsummer Night's Dream* (Shakespeare's Globe); *Windibops* (UK Tour); *Tyrannosaurus Drip* (Stratford Circus); *Love's Labour's Lost* (Shakespeare's Globe); *Tanika's Journey* and *Invisible* (Deafinitely Theatre); *Girls And Dolls* (Southwark Playhouse); *Deafhood* (Bristol Old Vic) and *I Believe In Unicorns* and *We're Going On A Bear Hunt* (Little Angel Theatre).

Other credits include: *Scrooge* (D-Live!); *Midnight Movie* (R&D); *Sonnet 18* (Short Film); *Dorothy Miles* (Television); *Diana and the Gods from Galatea* (R&D); *Extraordinary Wall of Silence* (R&D); *Silent Shakespeare* (Workshop, Old Vic); *Sonnet 30* (Short Film); *Margaret Ashman Gallery* (Still Photography); *The Hub* (Television); *BSL Zone Showcase* (Internet); *Snapshot Dicing with Sex* (Documentary); *All Day* (Short Film) and *Wicked* series 2 & 3 (Television).

Charmaine Wombwell

Charmaine studied Drama at the University of Hull before fronting and also writing for original music projects for several years. In 2013 she began her training in Physical Theatre & Devising at the London International School of Performing Arts (LISPA), and soon after created her one-woman dark clown show, *Scarlet Shambles: It Used to be Me*, for the Edinburgh Fringe 2015, and Tellit, Shambala and Barcelona Solo festivals culminating with Stratford Circus' International Women's Day Festival (2016). Charmaine then returned to LISPA (now in Berlin) to study Integral Movement and Performance Practice, to deepen her understanding of storytelling and artistic creation. Other performance credits include *Grounded* (Park Theatre/Deafinitely Theatre); *Champion of the World* (BSLBT BSLZone/Film4); *Karagula* (Soho Theatre); *The Listening Room* (Old Red Lion); *Not I* (BSL performance for Touretteshero/Battersea Arts Centre and tour: Southbank Centre, Albany Deptford, The Lowry (Salford), DADA Fest (Liverpool)); *Fram and Dunt* (Push Festival, HOME Manchester). Voice over credits: Aimee in *Magic Hands* (Cbeebies). Directing credits include Raymond Antrobus' *A Language We Both Know How To Sound Out* (Roundhouse). Charmaine is very excited to be starting work on *Going Through* at Bush Theatre, especially as it is where she did her work experience as a teenager many years ago...

Creative Team

Estelle Savasta – Playwright
Estelle is a French writer and director, and founder of the theatre company *Hippolyte a mal au cœur*. Her first production as a director for the company was *Le Grand Cahier (The Notebook)* by Agota Kristof, presented in a bilingual staging (French and Sign Language) in 2005. She wrote and directed the company's second production, *Seule dans ma peau d'âne (Alone in my Donkey Skin)* which was nominated for a Moliere Award in 2008.

After working with the *International Visual Theatre* in Paris, integrating French and Sign Language, she wrote and directed *Traversée (Going Through)* in 2011. The play was translated into English and Spanish and has received multiple productions in France, Canada and will be soon produced in Mexico.

Kirsten Hazel Smith – Translator
Kirsten Hazel Smith grew up in France to Scottish parents, and trained as an actor at the Royal Conservatoire of Scotland. As well as *Going Through*, Kirsten has translated Estelle Savasta's *Lettres Jamais Ecrites* for the Cross Channel Theatre Group, and *What World Do I Live In? Dialogues Without Borders* for Boundless Theatre and Théâtre de la Cité, Toulouse.

Kirsten is a bilingual reader for the Cross Channel Theatre Group which promotes French new writing in the UK.

Omar Elerian – Director
Omar is an award winning Italian/Palestinian theatre director, deviser and performer, who trained at Jacques Lecoq International Theatre School in Paris. He joined the Bush in 2012 alongside Madani Younis and since then has been the resident Associate Director. He is in charge of the Bush's talent development, leading on the Associate Artists and Project 2036 schemes. He is also involved in the development and delivery of the Bush's artistic program and lead the programming of the RADAR festival between 2012 and 2015. His directing credits for the Bush include gig theatre sensation

Misty by Arinzé Kene, the Edinburgh Fringe First – winning *NASSIM* by Nassim Soleimanpour, *One Cold Dark Night* by Nancy Harris and *Islands* by Caroline Horton. As Associate Director, he has worked alongside Madani Younis on the Bush's productions of *Leave Taking*, *The Royale*, *Perseverance Drive* and *Chalet Lines*. Other credits include acclaimed site-specific production *The Mill – City of Dreams*, Olivier Award nominated *You're Not Like The Other Girls Chrissy* (Edinburgh Festival and on Tour), *Testa di Rame* (Italy), *Les P'tites Grandes Choses* (France) and *L'Envers du Décor* (France).

Louise Stern – Associate Director
California born, London based artist and writer Louise Stern uses various forms of language to explore communication and isolation. Attending the California School for the Deaf, Fremont, Stern grew up in an exclusively deaf community (fourth generation deaf on her father's side, and third generation on her mother's side) and saw in literature and visual language a way to investigate and liberate. Graduating from Gallaudet University, Washington DC in 2000 as the only student studying art history before moving to London to read an MA at Sotheby's three years later, Stern went on to work as an assistant to filmmaker and photographer Sam Taylor-Johnson. As an artist Stern's works have been exhibited in Geneva, Madrid, Barcelona, Istanbul, Paris, and London among other places. In 2018, she was awarded an art residency by the University of Manchester.

As a writer she was the founder and publisher of *Maurice* 2002-2009, a contemporary art magazine for children. Her work at *Maurice* led to her collection of short stories, *Chattering*, published by Granta in 2011 (long-listed for the Frank O'Connor Short Story Award); and novel *Ismael and His Sisters*, published by the same in 2015 (long-listed for the Warwick Prize). Her creative writing has been commissioned by publications including Granta Magazine, the Garage Museum of Contemporary Art, the Royal Academy Magazine, and Radio 4.

Stern has also employed other mediums including dance and film in her practice. In 2018, she wrote and directed a short film, *BOAT* for Film 4.

Rajha Shakiry – Designer

Rajha is a freelance theatre designer and maker, who works across the spectrum of scripted and devised theatre, dance, musical theatre, and opera. She was born in Iraq and educated in England, completing a degree in Mathematics before re-training in Theatre Design at Wimbledon School of Art (BA) and Royal Central School of Speech and Drama (MA, distinction). Rajha's work has most recently been exhibited at the V&A (*Make:Believe*, 2015) and as a World Stage Design 2013 finalist.

Recent projects include: *Nine Night* (National Theatre); *Misty* (Bush Theatre); *The Dark* (Fuel); *The Mountaintop* (Young Vic/ JMK); *Mobile* (The Paper Birds); *Richard II* (Shakespeare's Globe); *The Head Wrap Diaries* (The Place, Uchenna Dance); *I Stand Corrected* and *Muhammad Ali & Me* (both Mojisola Adebayo). Rajha's current collaborations include work at National Theatre and Royal Court Theatre.

Nina Dunn – Video Designer

Nina designs video and projections for a wide range of shows, working internationally across theatre, opera, dance, immersive, live events and public art.

Recent work for theatre includes: *9 to 5* (Savoy Theatre, London); *The Box of Delights* (Wilton's Music Hall); *Contagion* (Shobana Jeyasingh Dance); *Copenhagen, Fiddler on the Roof, Forty Years On* (Chichester Festival Theatre); *Miss Littlewood, The Seven Acts of Mercy, Volpone* (RSC); *Der Freischütz, Macbeth* (Vienna State Opera); *The Damned United* (West Yorkshire Playhouse/Tour); *The Assassination of Katie Hopkins* (Theatr Clwyd); *Cookies* (Theatre Royal Haymarket); *The Rocky Horror Show* (European tour); *The Life, The Diary of a Teenage Girl* (Southwark Playhouse); *The Mountaintop* (Young Vic and UK Tour); *No Man's Land* (Tour/West End).

Immersive and live events include: *Spring Gala* (Royal Opera House); *Alice's Adventures Underground 2015* (Les Enfants Terribles/EBP); *Back to the Future, Grand Budapest Hotel, Miller's Crossing* and *Who Framed Roger Rabbit* for Secret Cinema.

Josh Pharo – Lighting Designer

Joshua works as a Lighting and Projection Designer across theatre, dance, opera, music, film & art installation. Most recently Joshua has won two awards at the Theatre and Technology Awards 2018; Creative Innovation in Lighting Design for *The Claim* at Shoreditch Town Hall and Creative Innovation in Video Projection Design for *The Shape of the Pain* at Battersea Arts Centre. He was nominated for Knight of Illumination Award 2017 for his work on *Removal Men*.

Current and forthcoming projects include: *The Ridiculous Darkness* (Gate Theatre); *Noughts & Crosses* (UK Tour); *The Color Purple* (Leicester Curve / Birmingham Hippodrome) and Vassa (Almeida).

Recent credits include: *Counting Sheep* (Belarus Free Theatre); *The Wolves* (Stratford East); *OthelloMacbeth* (Lyric Hammersmith; HOME Manchester); *Future Bodies* (HOME Manchester); *100: Unearth* (Wildworks); *Nanjing* (Sam Wanamaker Playhouse); *Double Vision* (Wales Millenium Centre); *Random/Generations* (Chichester Festival Theatre); TRUST (Gate Theatre); *The Shape of the Pain* (China Plate Theatre; Fringe First Winner, BAC).

Elena Peña – Sound Designer

Elena is an Associate Artist for Inspector Sands where her credits include: *The Lounge* (Summer Hall, Edinburgh – Offie Nomination for Best Sound Design); *Mass Observation* (Almeida Theatre); *Rock Pool*, *Seochon Odyssey* (HiSeoul Festival, Korea) and *A High Street Odyssey* (UK tour, National Theatre Watch This Space Festival).

Other theatre credits include: *Misty* (Bush Theatre/West End); *Islands* and *Hir* (Bush Theatre); *The Remains Of the Day* (Royal and Derngate); *Sällskapsrummet* (Riksteatern, Sweden); *The Wizard of Oz* (Pitlochry Festival Theatre); *Thick as Thieves* (Clean Break/Theatre Clwyd); *Double Vision* (Wales Millennium Centre); *Mountains: The Dreams of Lily Kwok* (Manchester Royal Exchange, UK tour); *All Of Me* (China Plate); *How I Hacked My Way Into Space* (Unlimited Theatre, Latitude Festival and tour); *The Caretaker* (Bristol Old Vic); *Thebes*

Land (Arcola); *Years of Sunlight* (Theatre 503); *The Bear/ The Proposal* (Young Vic); *Brainstorm* (Company3, National Theatre); *The Christians, I Call My Brothers, The Iphigenia Quartet, Unbroken* (Gate Theatre);*The Village Social* (National Theatre Wales) and *Sleepless* (Shoreditch Town Hall, Analogue Theatre, Staatstheater Mainz).

Radio includes: *12 Years, The Meet Cute, Duchamps Urinal* (BBC Radio 4).

Sound installations include: *Have Your Circumstances Changed?* and *Yes These Eyes Are The Windows* (ArtAngel).

Laura Salmi – Video Design Assistant
Laura is a freelance filmmaker working in theatre and video ethnography. She has previously worked as a TV producer and documentary maker in the fields of music and the arts.

Recent theatre projects as a video design assistant and co-ordinator include: *9to5* (Savoy Theatre); *In the Night Garden Live* (2019 UK Tour); *The House on Cold Hill* (UK Tour); *The Box of Delights* (Wilton's Music Hall); *Contagion* (Shobana Jeyasingh Dance) and *Spring Gala* (Royal Opera House).

Alex Horner – Costume Supervisor
Alex Horner is a freelance costume supervisor and wardrobe manager. He studied Creative Arts for Theatre and Film (BA) at the University for the Creative Arts before developing a career in theatre wardrobe since 2010.

Recent costume supervisor projects include: *Sundowning* (UK tour) and *The Mountaintop* (UK tour). Work in wardrobe include: *The Rocky Horror Show* (UK tour); *Misty* (Trafalgar Studios); *The Bodyguard* (China tour); *Sunny Afternoon* (UK tour); *Priscilla Queen of the Desert* (UK tour); *Top Hat* (UK tour); *Wicked* (West End) and Glyndebourne Festival Opera. He has also worked as a Head of Wardrobe for the English National Ballet School.

Emily Aboud – Assistant Director
Emily is a theatre director born and raised in Trinidad and Tobago. She is an associate artist at the Bush Theatre for

Project 2036. Past directing work includes: *A Place for We* (Rich Mix); *What we talk about when we (don't) talk about race* (Theatre503) and *Ma Am I Good?* (Leicester Square Theatre).

Past work as assistant director includes: *Deposit* (Hampstead Theatre); *Child of the Divide* (Polka Theatre and UK Tour) and *A Small Place* (Gate Theatre). She is the artistic director of lagahoo productions, a company focused on Caribbean new writing, and performs regularly as a drag king.

Phil Buckley – Production Manager
Phil is a north-west based Production Manager who has worked on shows in the West End and has managed tours across the UK and the world.

Previous work includes: Production Managing for Nimax Theatres, Emma Brunjes Productions, Hull UK City of Culture, Hull Truck, LGBT History Month, Inkbrew Productions, Bound & Gagged, Trans Creative, Switchflicker Productions, Contact Theatre, Manchester Metropolitan University, SH!T Theatre, Gag Reflex and Youth Music Theatre.

Phil has recently Production Managed Hull Truck's production of *Our Mutual Friend* which as commissioned as part of Hull's celebration of being City of Culture and the hugely popular *Rent Party* at The Crucible in Sheffield which is still touring. Also still touring is Kate O'Donnell's *You've Changed* which is a show about Kate's transition as a transgender woman.

Phil also works with highly acclaimed circus theatre group Ockham's Razor and has toured around Europe with their spectacular show *Tipping Point*.

Phil's tour managing experience for comedy acts include: UK tours of The Lost Voice Guy, Tape Face, Axis of Awesome and Sean Kelly &The Stars of Storage Hunters. Phil spent nearly two years working with Tape Face touring around Europe with two separate West End shows which Phil also designed the lighting for.

Patricia Davenport – Stage Manager

Patricia is a freelancer stage manager, originally from London, where she trained at Mountview Academy of Theatre Arts.

Recent work includes: *String Quartets Guide to Sex and Anxiety* (Birmingham Rep European tour); *Ubumuntu Arts Festival* (Rwanda); *Up n Under* (fingersmiths, UK tour); *Richard II* with David Tennant, *Henry IV pt I and 2, Henry V* (RSC, China, Hong Kong and Brooklyn NY); *Reasons to be Cheerful* (Graeae, UK tour); *Brief Encounter* (Kneehigh, UK tour); *What Fatima Did...* (Derby Theatre); *House of Bernarda Alba* (Royal Exchange Manchester); *The Who's Tommy* (Ramps on the Moon UK tour); *Julius Caesar* (RSC, Moscow, Ohio, New York); *The Winters Tale* (RSC, UK tour).

Jacob Amos – Assistant Stage Manager

Jacob Amos trained the Liverpool Institute for Performing Arts with a degree in Theatre and Performance Technology.

He has been working mainly as an Assistant Stage Manager since then and his credits include: *Blue Door* (Theatre Royal Bath); *The Things We Wouldn't Otherwise* Find (Leeds Playhouse); *4.48 Psychosis* (Deafinitely Theatre); The *Girl on the Train* (West Yorkshire Playhouse); *Wake* (Birmingham Opera Company); *Party Skills for the End of the World* (Manchester International Festival); *The Star* and *Quantum* (Liverpool Everyman and Playhouse).

Thank You's

A big thank you to the following organisations and individuals for making this show possible:

Mel, Lucy and all the team of the White City Youth Theatre
Dominic Glynn
Durham Marenghi and Clay Paky
Jeremy Roberts and ETC
Dan Last and White Light
The Gate
RT Scenic
Kay Buckley at the Bolton Octagon
Deafinitely Theatre

The production is generously supported by Margaret Guido's Charitable Trust and the AHRC Literature under Constraint network.

Bush Theatre

Bush Theatre

We make theatre
for London. Now.

The Bush is a world-famous home for new plays
and an internationally renowned champion of
playwrights. We discover, nurture and produce
the best new writers from the widest range of
backgrounds from our home in a distinctive corner
of west London.

The Bush has won over 100 awards and developed
an enviable reputation for touring its acclaimed
productions nationally and internationally.

We are excited by exceptional new voices,
stories and perspectives – particularly those with
contemporary bite which reflect the vibrancy of
British culture now.

Located in the newly renovated old library on
Uxbridge Road in the heart of Shepherd's Bush,
the theatre houses two performance spaces, a
rehearsal room and the lively Library Bar.

 Supported by **ARTS COUNCIL ENGLAND** h&f hammersmith & fulham

bushtheatre.co.uk

THANK YOU

The Bush Theatre would like to thank all its supporters whose valuable contributions have helped us to create a platform for our future and to promote the highest quality new writing, develop the next generation of creative talent, lead innovative community engagement work and champion diversity.

LONE STAR
Gianni Alen-Buckley
Michael Alen-Buckley
Rafael & Anne-Helene Biosse Duplan
Alice Findlay
Charles Holloway
Miles Morland

HANDFUL OF STARS
Dawn & Gary Baker
Charlie Bigham
Judy Bollinger
Clive & Helena Butler
Grace Chan
Clare & Chris Clark
Clyde Cooper
Sue Fletcher
Richard & Jane Gordon
Priscilla John
Simon & Katherine Johnson
Philippa Seal & Philip Jones QC
Joanna Kennedy
V&F Lukey
Robert Ledger & Sally Mousdale
Georgia Oetker
Philip & Biddy Percival
Clare Rich
Joana & Henrik Schliemann
Lesley Hill & Russ Shaw
van Tulleken Family
and one anonymous donor.

RISING STARS
ACT IV
Nicholas Alt
Mark Bentley
David Brooks
Catharine Browne
Matthew Byam Shaw
Tim & Andrea Clark
Sarah Clarke
Claude & Susie Cochin de Billy
Lois Cox
Susie Cuff
Matthew Cushen
Philippa Dolphin
John Fraser
Jack Gordon & Kate Lacy
Hugh & Sarah Grootenhuis
Jessica Ground
Thea Guest
Patrick Harrison
Ann & Ravi Joseph
Davina & Malcolm Judelson
Miggy Littlejohns
Isabella Macpherson

RISING STARS (continued)
Liz & Luke Mayhew
Michael McCoy
Judith Mellor
Caro Millington
Dan & Laurie Mucha
Mark & Anne Paterson
Pippa Prain
Barbara Prideaux
Emily Reeve
Renske & Marion
Sarah Richards
Susie Saville Sneath
Saleem & Alexandra Siddiqi
Brian Smith
Peter Tausig
Guy Vincent & Sarah Mitchell
Trish Wadley
Amanda Waggott
Alison Winter
and three anonymous donors.

SPONSORS & SUPPORTERS
AKA
Alen-Buckley LLP
Gianni & Michael Alen-Buckley
Jeremy Attard Manche
Bill & Judy Bollinger
Edward Bonham Carter
Martin Bowley
Duke & Duchess of Buccleuch
The Hon Mrs Louise Burness
Sir Charles & Lady Isabella Burrell
Philip & Tita Byrne
CHK Charities Limited
Peppe & Quentin Ciardi
Joanna & Hadyn Cunningham
Leo & Grega Daly
Patrick & Mairead Flaherty
Sue Fletcher
The Hon Sir Rocco Forte
The Hon Portia Forte
Mark Franklin
The Gatsby Charitable Foundation
The Right Hon Piers Gibson
Farid & Emilie Gragour
Victoria Gray
John Gordon
Vivienne Guinness
Melanie Hall
The Headley Trust
Brian Heyworth
Lesley Hill & Russ Shaw
Michael Holland & Denise O'Donoghue

SPONSORS & SUPPORTERS (continued)
Charles Holloway
Graham & Amanda Hutton
James Gorst Architects Ltd.
Simon & Katherine Johnson
Tarek & Diala Khlat
Bernard Lambilliotte
Marion Lloyd
The Lord Forte Foundation
Peter & Bettina Mallinson
Mahoro Charitable Trust
James Christopher Miller
Mitsui Fodosan (U.K.) Ltd
Alfred Munkenbeck III
Nick Hern Books
Georgia Oetker
RAB Capital
Kevin Pakenham
Sir Howard Panter
Joanna Prior
Josie Rourke
Lady Susie Sainsbury
Barry Serjent
Tim & Catherine Score
Search Foundation
Richard Sharp
Susie Simkins
Edward Snape & Marilyn Eardley
Michael & Sarah Spencer
Stanhope PLC
Ross Turner
The Syder Foundation
van Tulleken Family
Johnny & Dione Verulam
Robert & Felicity Waley-Cohen
Elizabeth Wigoder
Philip Wooller
Danny Wyler
and three anonymous donors.

TRUSTS AND FOUNDATIONS
The Andrew Lloyd Webber Foundation
The Boris Karloff Foundation
The Boshier-Hinton Foundation
The Bruce Wake Charitable Trust
The Chapman Charitable Trust
The City Bridge Trust
Cockayne—Grants for the Arts
The John S Cohen Foundation
The Daisy Trust
The Equity Charitable Trust
Esmée Fairbairn Foundation
Fidelio Charitable Trust
Foyle Foundation

TRUSTS AND FOUNDATIONS (continued)
Garfield Weston Foundation
Garrick Charitable Trust
Hammersmith United Charities
Heritage of London Trust
John Lyon's Charity
The J Paul Getty Jnr Charitable Trust
The John Thaw Foundation
The Kirsten Scott Memorial Trust
The Leverhulme Trust
The London Community Foundation
Margaret Guido's Charitable Trust
The Martin Bowley Charitable Trust
The Monument Trust
The Noel Coward Foundation
Paul Hamlyn Foundation
Peter Wolff Foundation
Pilgrim Trust
The Royal Victoria Hall Foundation
Sir John Cass's Foundation
Stavros Niarchos Foundation
The Theatres Trust
Viridor Credits
The Williams Charitable Trust
Western Riverside Worshipful Company of Mercers Environmental Fund
The Wolfson Foundation
and one anonymous donor.

CORPORATE SPONSORS AND MEMBERS
The Agency (London) Ltd
Dorsett Shepherds Bush
Drama Centre London
Fever Tree
The Groucho Club
THE HOXTON
Philip Wooller
Westfield London

PUBLIC FUNDING

Supported by
ARTS COUNCIL ENGLAND

hammersmith & fulham

If you are interested in finding out how to be involved, please visit **bushtheatre.co.uk/support-us** or email **development@bushtheatre.co.uk** or call **020 8743 3584**.

First published in April 2019 by Oberon Books Ltd
521 Caledonian Road, London N7 9RH
Tel: +44 (0) 20 7607 3637 / Fax: +44 (0) 20 7607 3629
e-mail: info@oberonbooks.com
www.oberonbooks.com

A catalogue record for this book is available from the British Library.

PB ISBN: 9781786827579
E ISBN: 9781786827586

Cover Design by Studio Doug; Photography by Bronwen Sharp

Printed and bound by 4EDGE Limited, Hockley, Essex, UK.
eBook conversion by Lapiz Digital Services, India.

Visit www.oberonbooks.com to read more about all our books and to buy them. You will
also find features, author interviews and news of any author events, and you can sign up for
e-newsletters so that you're always first to hear about our new releases.

Printed on FSC® accredited paper

10 9 8 7 6 5 4 3 2 1

Characters

NOUR
YOUMNA

Writer's note:

Youmna is deaf and communicates using sign language. The first French production of 'Going Through' ('Traversée') was created as an entirely bilingual French and French Sign Language performance.

In this edition, sometimes Nour narrates on her own; sometimes Nour and Youmna narrate in their respective languages and this forms two parallel accounts; and sometimes Youmna signs to Nour, and Nour speaks the words.

Nour speaks like a jittery bird; fast, not really thinking about what she is saying.

However, the text is written in such a way that the director can decide to only take into account Nour's story. In this case the play can be considered as a monologue.

Part I

1.

NOUR

Youmna is beautiful.

She is gentle.

Youmna is good and she smells like the wind.

Youmna is not my mother and I would like her to be.

Nour and Youmna are narrating their story, each in her own language.

NOUR and YOUMNA

Youmna's ears don't work.
My ears don't work.

She was born like that.
I was born like that.

Youmna is teaching me her language.
I am teaching Nour my language.

And this language belongs only to us.
And this language belongs only to us.

I like this.
She likes this.

My name is Nour.
My name is Youmna.

NOUR

Youmna says that I am the Nour of her life, even if her tummy never carried me.

2.

Morning in a tiny little house.

Two twin beds. Nour and Youmna are sat pressed up against each other, in one of the beds. They are performing a sequence of signs and numbers in time together. Like a joyous ritual. A bit like a game of rock-paper-scissors. They stop at the same time. They get out of bed.

3.

In the tiny little house. Youmna is sat at the edge of one of the beds. Nour is sat at her feet on a mat.

Youmna signs. Nour speaks the words.

NOUR and YOUMNA

Youmna says that my mother was also beautiful, gentle and good.
Your mother was also beautiful, gentle and good.

She says that my mother was her friend.
Your mother was my friend.

2

The only person to have learnt her language.
The only person to have learnt my language.

Just like that, for no reason, so as to be her friend.
Just like that, for no reason, so as to be my friend.

It surprised them both.
It surprised us both.

She says We laughed about nothing, and made each other silly promises.
We laughed about nothing, and made each other silly promises.

She says To be someone, sometimes, you need to be more than one.
To be someone, sometimes, you need to be more than one.

And there were two of us.
And there were two of us.

Nour and Youmna speak, each in her own language.

NOUR and YOUMNA

Me, I don't want to know anything.
Nour doesn't want to know anything.

In this life, I only want Youmna.
She says that in this life she only wants me.

So I say nothing.
So she says nothing.

I only have Youmna and she is the Nour of my life.
She says that she only has me and that I am the Nour of her life.

Even if she is not my mother.
Even if I am not her mother.

And even if her name is Youmna.

And even if my name is Youmna.

4.

Evening. In the tiny little house.

Youmna, right at the edge of Nour's bed. Nour right at the edge of sleep. Youmna makes shadow puppets with her signs. She is telling a story. Then she turns off the light and with it, the shadows. With her finger she traces a circle on Nour's forehead and a circle in the palm of her hand. Nour falls asleep.

5.

Nour and Youmna speak, each in her own language.

NOUR and YOUMNA

Youmna never speaks about my father.

Nour never asks any questions about her father.

That suits me.

That suits me.

It's already complicated enough as it is.

It's already complicated enough as it is.

6.

Morning in the tiny little house. Nour and Youmna are sat pressed up against each other, in one of the beds. Through Youmna's signing we recognise the joyous ritual from before. Like a game of rock-paper-scissors.

NOUR and YOUMNA

We own.
We own.

1 tiny little house.
1 tiny little house.

1 bit of garden.
1 bit of garden.

1 tree.
1 tree.

2 beds.
2 beds.

4 blankets and 4 sheets.
4 blankets and 4 sheets.

2 mattresses and 2 pillows.
2 mattresses and 2 pillows.

1 mat.
1 mat.

2 saucepans and 1 pot.
2 saucepans and 1 pot.

4 plates and 3 matching glasses because I broke the fourth.
4 plates and 3 matching glasses because she broke the fourth.

1 teapot.
1 teapot.

12 assorted utensils that can be used to eat, serve or stir.
12 assorted utensils that can be used to eat, serve or stir.

2 toothbrushes.
2 toothbrushes.

1 hairbrush and 1 comb.
1 hairbrush and 1 comb.

2 towels.
2 towels.

1 green suitcase.
1 green suitcase.

4 complete outfits from head to toe including underwear.
4 complete outfits from head to toe including underwear.

1 metal dish for remedies.
1 metal dish for remedies.

2 pairs of shoes.
2 pairs of shoes.

1 shelf, 4 books, 1 tiny little box.
1 shelf, 4 books, 1 tiny little box.

We have everything we need.
Nour says we have everything we need.

We want for nothing.
That we want for nothing.

Everything in our house is of use.
That everything in our house is of use.

Except the little box.
Except the little box.

The little box is on the shelf. I am allowed to look at it and to
touch it.
The little box is on the shelf. She is allowed to look at it and to
touch it.

I am not allowed to open it.
She is not allowed to open it.

I promised.
She promised.

7.

Nour and Youmna speak, each in her own language.

NOUR and YOUMNA

Youmna knows how to ward off the evil eye and make burns
disappear.
I know how to ward off the evil eye and make burns disappear.

She knows how to talk to unruly children in their mothers'
tummies, and soothe hearts that beat too fast.
I know how to talk to unruly children in their mothers' tummies, and
soothe hearts that beat too fast.

She knows how to see into the future, if it doesn't go too far.
I know how to see into the future, if it doesn't go too far.

All the women from round here come to see her.
All the women from round here come to see me.

None have taken the trouble to learn her language but they all respect her. And Youmna gets by.
None have taken the trouble to learn my language but they all respect me. And I get by.

If you ask me, I think that with all her knowledge, she gives them the heebie-jeebies.
I think that with all my knowledge, I scare them a bit.

8.

Nour and Youmna speak, each in her own language.

NOUR and YOUMNA

I go to school.
I send Nour to school.

Youmna wants me to go so that I hear the language of others.
I want her to hear the language of others.

The one which is spoken with the mouth.
The one which is spoken with the mouth.

I learn words.
She learns words.

9.

In the tiny little house. Youmna is sat at the edge of one of the beds. Nour is sat by her feet on a mat.

Youmna signs. Nour speaks the words.

NOUR and YOUMNA

Youmna says The journey and you came about at the same time inside your mother's tummy.
The journey and you came about at the same time inside your mother's tummy.

As soon as she felt you there, she made a decision.
As soon as she felt you there, she made a decision.

Your mother said For me it's done. I can accept that.
Your mother said For me it's done. I can accept that.

Not for the child.
Not for the child.

She said I will work hard and my child will never go hungry.
She said I will work hard and my child will never go hungry.

My child will go to school, with her hair dishevelled if she likes.
My child will go to school, with her hair dishevelled if she likes.

One night, a few days after you were born, she came here.
One night, a few days after you were born, she came here.

She said I am leaving.
She said I am leaving.

The journey will be long and dangerous.
The journey will be long and dangerous.

I can't take the child with me.

I can't take the child with me.

I will leave first, when the nest is ready, promise that you'll let her come to me.

I will leave first, when the nest is ready, promise that you'll let her come to me.

Youmna says I promised. It was my last silly promise.

I promised. It was my last silly promise.

So your mother opened the palms of my hands, like this, and she lay you there. Tiny little fledgling.

So your mother opened the palms of my hands, like this, and she lay you there. Tiny little fledgling.

She said Keep her, protect her.

She said Keep her, protect her.

Lend her your tummy to sleep on. Love her.

Lend her your tummy to sleep on. Love her.

And she flew away.

And she flew away.

We went into my house.

We went into my house.

I lent you my tummy to sleep on.

I lent you my tummy to sleep on.

That's how it began, for you and me.

That's how it began, for you and me.

Nour and Youmna speak, each in her own language.

NOUR and YOUMNA

At this moment in the story vertigo always grabs hold of me.
At this moment in the story vertigo always grabs hold of Nour.

So I cover my eyes in Youmna's hair.
So she covers her eyes in my hair.

And I make endless lists.
And, inside, I know she makes endless lists.

Youmna says I mustn't tell anyone this story.
I tell her not to tell anyone this story.

So I keep my mouth shut.
It's a story just for us.

And we live with this omen over our two heads.
And we live with this omen over our two heads.

This woman who bore me will write.
Nour will grow up.

And I will have to leave Youmna and go.
And she will have to go.

10.

Nour and Youmna speak, each in her own language.

NOUR and YOUMNA

One day, for the girls, the school closed.
One day, for the girls, the school closed.

I didn't understand why.
Nour didn't understand why.

As if the men had become ogres,
As if the men had become ogres,

The women lowered their heads and hurried along.
The women lowered their heads and hurried along.

We stay in our tiny little house most of the time.
We stay in our tiny little house most of the time.

I learn history and grammar on the tips of Youmna's fingers.
Nour learns history and grammar on the tips of my fingers.

She is scared that I'll forget the language of others. The one with the mouth.
I am scared that she'll forget the language of others. Those who speak with their mouths.

She makes me say the words.
I make her say the words.

Not always, obviously.
Not always, obviously.

11.

Evening in the tiny little house.

Youmna right at the edge of Nour's bed. Nour right at the edge of sleep. Youmna makes shadow puppets with her signs. She is telling a story. Then she turns off the light and with it, the shadows. With her finger, she traces a circle on Nour's forehead, and a circle in the palm of her hand.

Nour and Youmna speak, each in her own language.

NOUR and YOUMNA

And then it happened, just before night, without warning.
And then it happened, I had to tell her.

Like every evening, Youmna and her orange tree body on the edge of my bed.
Like every evening, Nour and her Spring-like scent await sleep.

The story of the tiny little boy and the small stones.
I tell the story of the tiny little boy and the small stones.

Youmna's hand on my back as if she was smoothing out a beautiful, crumpled-up love letter.
My hand on her back as if I was smoothing out a beautiful, crumpled-up love letter.

And then, with her thumb, a circle in the palm of my hand and a circle on my forehead.
And then, with my thumb, a circle in the palm of her hand and a circle on her forehead.

But that evening her hand stops. It stays there.
But that evening my hand stops. It stays there.

Youmna's beautiful assured hand trembles.
My hand trembles, and I can't do anything about it.

Youmna signs. Nour speaks the words.

13

NOUR and YOUMNA

Youmna's says Your mother has written. She is waiting for you. She has everything organised.

Your mother has written. She is waiting for you. She has everything organised.

Nour and Youmna speak, each in her own language.

NOUR and YOUMNA

It's like a slap in the face.

For Nour, it's like a slap in the face.

And with slaps, there is nothing to be done.

And with slaps, there is nothing to be done.

Just wait for the burning on your cheek to die down.

Just wait for the burning on your cheek to die down.

That humiliation and anger can go on their merry way.

That humiliation and anger can go on their merry way.

12.

Night. Nour is alone in her bed. Youmna is outside the tiny little house.

Each speaks in her own language.

NOUR and YOUMNA

It's my last night in this bed.

It's her last night in that bed.

Sleep will not come. Vertigo is already here.

For me, sleep will not come and for Nour, I know it, vertigo is already here.

And so, I recite the list against fear, and the one against sadness, the list against impatience and the one against the things that we don't want to see coming.

And so, she recites the list against fear and the one against sadness, the list against impatience and the one against the things that we don't want to see coming.

2423 sensibly ordered words like little soldiers that know how to march in a straight line.

2423 sensibly ordered words like little soldiers that know how to march in a straight line.

2423 little soldiers that, tonight, have no use.

2423 little soldiers that, tonight, have no use.

13.

The following morning. The day breaks. Youmna gets up carefully without waking Nour. She heads for the mat and takes out a pair of scissors, which are hidden under it. Gently, she wakes Nour and invites her to sit close to her on the mat.

Youmna signs. Nour speaks the words.

NOUR and YOUMNA

She says Nour of my life, for this journey, you will need to be a boy.

Nour of my life, for this journey, you will need to be a boy.

I have neither the heart nor the words to tell you what can sometimes happen to girls.

I have neither the heart nor the words to tell you what can sometimes happen to girls.

It's not always children's stories that happen to children.

It's not always children's stories that happen to children.

And then, here, a girl on her own, would never be allowed to undertake the journey.

And then, here, a girl on her own, would never be allowed to undertake the journey.

She says, Nour of my life, you will be beautiful again.

Nour of my life, you will be beautiful again.

She says You will be handsome.

You will be handsome.

And that everything grows back, grass, desires, branches, and even hair.

And that everything grows back, grass, desires, branches, and even hair.

And over there, you will be allowed to wear disorder on your head.

And over there, you will be allowed to wear disorder on your head.

You will be beautiful, my big little one, you will be beautiful with your dishevelled hair.

You will be beautiful, my big little one, you will be beautiful with your dishevelled hair.

Youmna plaits Nour's hair. She cuts it. Nour runs her hands through her hair, all over, to feel the shortness of it.

NOUR

Now I have a birdie head.

14.

Youmna sits cross-legged on her bed. Nour, standing on the bed, plaits Youmna's hair.

Each speaks in her own language.

NOUR and YOUMNA

I leave tonight.
She leaves tonight.

We are trying hard to do everything the same.
We are trying hard to do everything the same.

The same gestures, the same everyday signs.
The same gestures, the same everyday signs.

But our gestures, our signs, are a little bit off.
But our gestures, our signs, are a little bit off.

As if, in a subtle way, the world had shifted.
As if, in a subtle way, the world had shifted.

Like the day is being torn apart.
Like the day is being torn apart.

I don't say anything.
Nour doesn't say anything.

Youmna can't say anything to me.
I can't say anything.

The knot is in our throats and in our hands.
The knot is in our throats and in our hands.

Tightening.
Tightening.

So, in order to do some good, while we still can.
So, in order to do some good, while we still can.

We make out as if nothing is happening.
We make out as if nothing is happening.

We sneak looks at each other.
We sneak looks at each other.

And we give each other our best smiles.
And we give each other our best smiles.

Nour finishes plaiting Youmna's hair. Youmna gets up and retrieves a little linen bag from underneath the bed. She takes out some boy's clothes, which she hands to Nour. Also some shoes. Nour gets off the bed and slips on the clothes and the shoes.

NOUR

And then, all of a sudden, everything accelerates.

There's a noise at the door, three sudden knocks.

Youmna goes towards the shelf and takes the little box from it. She sits on the mat and hurries for Nour to come and sit next to her.

Youmna signs. Nour speaks the words.

NOUR and YOUMNA

Youmna says Since the beginning of time, women have given their daughters a gift that they cannot open until the first day of their life as a woman.

Since the beginning of time, women have given their daughters a gift that they cannot open until the first day of their life as a woman.

For us, this means the day that we leave our homes for that of a man.

For us, this means the day that we leave our homes for that of a man.

For you it will be different.

For you it will be different.

Your mother did not fail to uphold this tradition. This tiny little box is yours.

Your mother did not fail to uphold this tradition. This tiny little box is yours.

Take it.

Take it.

I trust that you will be able to recognise that day, your first day as a woman.

I trust that you will be able to recognise that day, your first day as a woman.

Promise to open it on a happy day.

Promise to open it on a happy day.

And if, one day, on the journey that will lead you to your mother you have to give up everything, give up everything but don't give up this.

And if, one day, on the journey that will lead you to your mother you have to give up everything, give up everything but don't give up this.

You have there the entire female lineage that came before you.

You have there the entire female lineage that came before you.

Promise to stay true to yourself.

Promise to stay true to yourself.

NOUR

I didn't understand, but I promised.

Youmna signs. Nour speaks the words.

NOUR and YOUMNA

Youmna says The car is waiting for you, my handsome boy.

The car is waiting for you, my handsome boy.

She also says, I love you like it's not possible.

I love you like it's not possible.

Nour takes the little box. She puts it in the linen bag.

She puts the bag on her shoulders.

They go out.

20

Part II

NOUR

I didn't turn around.

I didn't watch her become smaller and smaller.

There are certain things you can't watch disappearing without the risk of disappearing yourself.

And I know that she prefers it like this.

That she watches me knowing that I won't turn around.

The journey began at the precise moment when I couldn't feel her gaze on my back.

I turned around.

The road had swallowed up Youmna and our tiny little house, our bit of garden, our tree, our two beds, our four blankets and our four sheets, our two mattresses and our two pillows, our mat, our two saucepans and our pot, our four plates, and our three glasses, our teapot, our 12 assorted utensils, our comb, our brush, our two towels, our green suitcase, our metal dish, our shelf and our four books. The road had swallowed up everything.

Except the little box.

The man driving has a frank smile. He says to me Don't be scared little bird. You'll be okay.

And over there, it's so beautiful, that you'll forget.

At least, I now know, I really do look like a bird.

But I won't forget anything. I swear.

I swear it to the wind, to the sand, to the night, to the emptiness, to my shoes, to my little box. I swear it to everything that my eyes can cling onto and that I recognise. I swear it.

The man with the frank smile says, I have a cassette tape for little birds like you that leave their nests looking sorry for themselves.

Listen to this, little one. And when you get out of the car, if you like, you can take it with you.

It will do you some good when you miss listening to your mother sing.

I want to scream at him the mother I chose for myself sings only with her fingers, we didn't need music to fill the silence in our tiny little house and I'll always miss that and there's nothing that can change that. He doesn't need to have invented oranges to understand this. I would like him to be quiet and to leave my ears in peace.

But he turns to me, and smiles. A frank smile, there's nothing to be said, there's nothing like it to make you zip-it.

So I keep my tongue snug in my birdie head.

Then I realise that I don't know where the car is taking me.

I only know what I am leaving behind and nothing of what is to come.

2.

NOUR

We drive on.

If I close my eyes, I see Youmna.

Standing rigid on our bit of garden, she hasn't moved.

In my head, Youmna is statufied.

The day breaks.

The man with the frank smile says that we have left the country.

Inside I make lists faster and faster.

It doesn't work.

We arrive at a town.

The car stops.

3.

NOUR

I follow the man with the frank smile into a cafe.

We sit right at the back.

He orders two too strong teas, which we drink in silence.

He's understood that I wanted him to leave my ears in peace.

Then he says, I'm off, little bird.

Wait here. It shouldn't be long.

Someone will come and get you for the rest of the journey.

Don't worry, your mother has paid for everything until you get to your destination.

Don't worry.

He ruffles his hand through my hair, pays for the two too strong teas and heads for the door.

The moment he's through the door I want to yell at him how funny he is with his lousy sentences, leaving me on my own in a cafe full of men, where no one speaks my language, where no one looks remotely like a child, a girl or a woman. He leaves me on my own in a town, in a country whose name I don't even know, in a world, a universe, a galaxy of which I know nothing. Should he have a solution, a method, a plan so as not to worry, I'd quite like to know it, because me, here, right now, I can't see it.

But he turns back, gives me one last frank smile and makes me zip-it one last time.

4.

NOUR

The dirty clock dilly-dallies.

Time stretches out like a cat that has slept too much.

I try not to imagine what my life would become if no one came to get me.

It must happen, leaving a child in a cafe like a basket of vegetables at the market.

I close my eyes.

Youmna has still not moved.

Maybe she will never move again.

Her feet will take root. Her arms will turn as dry as old branches.

Maybe even her blood will turn to sap.

Who will know? Who will understand? Who would be surprised to see a new tree grow so quickly in our garden? No one.

I attempt to make a list to save me from vertigo.

It doesn't work.

5.

Night.

In front of the cafe, Nour is lying on the floor, wrapped around her linen bag. She is sleeping.

Youmna appears in front of her house, standing rigid in her bit of garden.

Slowly she becomes a tree.

Then, she appears next to Nour, sits next to her and signs over her sleeping face. A mixture of signs that speak of love, watermelons and moustaches. Then, with her thumb, she traces a circle on Nour's forehead, and a circle in the palm of Nour's hand. She disappears.

6.

NOUR

He's come in.

He's come to get me.

He didn't say hello, and didn't say sorry for being 31 hours late.

I followed him.

7.

NOUR

On the bus, there's an empty seat next to a man I find very handsome because he doesn't have a beard and the skin on his cheeks seems soft.

I sit down next to him.

I don't know if it's a good thing to have a father, but if you ask me when you stumble across a man like this, it can't be that bad.

The bus stops often. Men get on. They have moustaches and guns.

They get on, and can make us get off.

I don't know what happens once they make you get off, but if you ask me, judging by the look on everyone's face, it's not fun.

In any case, those that got off never got back on.

I don't see the point of these festive looking buses if it's just to let on gloomy-faced moustached men.

At the third stop, I pretend to be asleep. Peering through the tiny slit of my closed eyes, I watch the moustached men.

There are three of them.

The smallest looks meanly at the man I find handsome. If you ask me, that little one is hard as nails.

He approaches me.

My heart is beating so hard that you must be able to see it through my shirt.

He says words in his language to the man I find handsome. I don't understand these words, but it doesn't sound like he is asking for tips on how to grow tomatoes.

The man I find handsome calmly hands over his papers and puts his right arm around my shoulders.

It's the first time a man has ever touched me. I've got such a cramp in my heart, I feel like I might die, but that's not really the issue here.

The real issue is to find out whether the moustached men are going to make me get off the bus.

The small hard as nails man looks at the papers and immediately his face changes. He smiles, his smile doesn't suit him at all. It's as if someone else's smile has been stuck on his face.

He indicates to the other two that the inspection is done.

They get off and the bus leaves.

The man I find very handsome takes his arm away. I open my eyes.

He smiles at me and says to me in the language of my country, They really are stupid these moustached men.

I think that without him, I would have known once and for all what happens to those that are made to get off the bus.

8.

NOUR

At the last stop, I get off.

A small man with a huge belly comes towards me.

He takes me to a lorry full of watermelons.

I'm like a parcel that gets shipped from place to place.

You don't really ask a parcel their opinion about the situation.

I can't see the countryside. I am hot. I'm dying of thirst in amongst these water-bearing fruit.

The woman I am going to meet must have imagined I'd be travelling like a princess. The truth is I'm travelling like a watermelon.

9.

The sun hasn't yet risen when they come to get me.

They are five men.

The trafficker and four others, like me, en route to another place.

We walk all day long.

Sometimes a man stops by a tree and urinates.

I don't know how to do that.

I would need to hide behind a bush.

But if someone discovers that I'm a girl, I think very bad things would happen.

I won't tell you the rest of that day.

It feels hot and then it feels cold.

I walk head down at the back of the group and no one notices anything.

10.

NOUR

In the middle of the night, I recognise a familiar sound.

It is the sound of a man shooting at another.

I don't see whose enemy I could be, on the border of two countries I don't know.

We run like headless chickens for a while, which to me feels like an eternity.

Then the gunshots stop. The guide stops.

We stop.

We've crossed the border. We're safe.

One is missing.

No one says anything but everyone has noticed.

So no one rejoices at crossing this border.

No one rejoices at having dodged the bullets.

We look for sleep.

A group brought together silently by the night and a strange sort of guilty sadness.

And then, without even thinking about it, I sing a sweet, but not sad, lullaby for the one who didn't get through.

11.

We've been lying down a long time when we hear footsteps.

He is here.

It's not a joke: he is here.

He has made it through. He must have fallen, and then must have hidden, he must have lost our trail and then looked for us. We'll never know. But we do know that he is here.

I laugh. I laugh like a goat, like an idiot, like a camel.

I laugh at seeing this man alive.

I laugh at being alive too.

The guide doesn't try to shut me up. On this side of the border you can laugh in peace.

So the others laugh like me.

We pat him on the back. We clap our hands.

We celebrate this unknown man like a king.

We each tell jokes in our own languages, nobody understands anything, but that night, we couldn't care less.

12.

In a town on the coast, I wait for my next trafficker.

One evening, a very young man is waiting for me in front of
the hotel. He says Stop waiting for him, he won't come. I'm
going tonight, come with me, if you want. He takes me to the
port. He gives me a plank of wood. He says the hardest thing
is to hold on. We wait crouching down by the side of the road
like warriors. He spots a stopped red lorry, he says Go.

13.

One day I arrived.

I mean to say I was there.

No one left to wait for. No one waiting for me either.

I walk for days, nights, months without knowing where to
or why.

I can't seem to find the woman who bore me.

Life in general already requires too much strength without
having to look for a mother too.

One day, I meet a woman from this new country. She takes
me to a place where, for the first time since I left, I can tell her
what happened. An interpreter translates. It's painful, but it
feels good.

Part III

1.

NOUR

I am in a home for adolescents.

I go to school.

In Mrs. Prune's class we speak 12 different languages. Let's just say she can't be short of ideas, and she needs ironclad nerves.

She needs to be super clever.

Mrs. Prune is super clever.

2.

NOUR

I have to go for a medical check-up. I need to strip naked. To be checked all over. I have never been naked in front of anyone before. I cry for seven whole nights.

That day, in everyone's eyes I become a girl again. Needless to say, I change bedrooms.

In any case, it would have become obvious eventually. There are certain things that you can't hide, if you know what I mean.

3.

In the home. Nour is in her bed, asleep.

Youmna appears. A sorrowful smile. With her thumb she traces a circle on Nour's forehead and one in the palm of Nour's hand. She disappears.

4.

NOUR

Now, I share a bedroom with four girls. The one who sleeps the closest to me is sensational.

We don't talk about our previous lives. We don't talk about our parents. That way, we avoid the nightmares.

However, I feel that silently we are friends.

5.

NOUR

One day, all those who have come from afar are called in to have X-rays taken of their wrists and hips.

They explain that it's to find out our ages.

My new friend is the same age as me. She swears it to me, she cries, snivels, snot dribbles down her face. Nevertheless, the X-Ray says she's an adult and they agree with the X-Ray even though everyone knows that often the X-Rays get it wrong. My friend leaves the home. First stop, the plane to take her back. There where she never wants to go back to, for reasons of her own and if you ask me that's fair enough.

I have too much anger to be sad.

Luckily they don't do X-Rays of our brains, because with all that we've seen since we left, we would all be at least 79 years old.

6.

NOUR

I've left Mrs. Prune's class and I go to college with the others.

The teachers say that I am exemplary, brave, and a bunch of words that parents love to hear. I'm not so sure I'm all those things, but learning everything off by heart until the cows go to bed is nearly as effective as making lists to fight against vertigo.

7.

Nour is becoming a young woman. Her hair is long.

I'm 18 and everything is becoming complicated. Maybe I'll get to stay, maybe I'll be sent back. It's a lottery, where I don't even get to choose the numbers.

We fill out the paperwork and we wait.

Whilst waiting, you absolutely have to steer clear of the police. And when you start getting scared, the police are everywhere.

I've found a solution. If the police are on the same side of the pavement as me, I go straight up to them as a young girl in my own right, and with an assured look in my eyes, I ask them for the time. I don't know if it's true but I imagine that: "Quarter to four and can I see your papers Miss?" would never be the response.

Whilst waiting, you also need to act as if nothing is happening, and prepare yourself for a future here as if you are certain you're staying.

One morning an educator asks me the question.

I say I want to help babies out of their mother's tummies.

She says Midwife. It's called a midwife.

Her smile and tone of voice aren't as usual. Like a tower that leans ever so slightly.

They enrol me in a school.

I learn the technical words and movements.

In the midst of this training I slightly forget the reality of my situation.

But one morning it catches the collar of my winter coat by surprise.

As an adult, without papers, I am not legally allowed to be enrolled at the school.

What a fuss it causes.

Both students and teachers protest for me in front of the school. People from everywhere write to the authorities.

I don't know why they are doing that. I don't even know them.

I want to disappear.

8.

NOUR

They were strong, they succeeded. I am allowed to stay here. To leave and come back.

With my residence card in my pocket, I go in search of police stations all day long, just so I can enjoy going in and asking them for the time without feeling my heart tremble.

9.

NOUR

The euphoria lasts a couple of days, and then one morning it's as if everything collapses on top of me all at once.

Now that I'm done with survival, everything catches up with me. Being snatched away, the journey, the ugly things I saw that I would never tell a soul about, the borders that go through our body, the stupid moustached men, the hours balancing under the lorry.

My existence has landed on top of me like a bad joke.

I do the midwife exam, like doing my teeth when I get up in the morning, without really thinking about it.

I pass without any joy. Still in this same state.

10.

In the home. Nour is fully dressed lying on her bed. We're not sure if she is asleep. Youmna appears as if she is walled-in. She signs to Nour for her to get up. She disappears. Nour gets up.

11.

NOUR

Some days, life takes a step forward. Today is one of those days.

This morning for the first time I'll be in the delivery room, as the midwife helping the baby into this world.

I go in.

The woman who is there is on her own. She looks at me like a fox caught in the headlights.

You won't believe me, but this woman speaks only one language and no other. Mine.

My childhood language, my neglected, forgotten and vanished language comes back to me, fluent and whole.

I place my hand on her forehead.

Nour signs then says:

Don't worry.

Everything will be ok.

I'll be here.

Listen to its heart beating.

Your child is coming.

You have the strength and you have the courage.

So does your baby.

It's looking for the path to daylight.

Feel.

You're taking steps together.

At dawn, when we greet its moist head into the light, I offer
the mother my most victorious smile.
And I say Rejoice, it's a girl.

It is a full day. A happy day.

My first day as a woman was at night.

I go home to open the little box.

12.

Early morning.

From under her pillow Nour takes out the little box.

*She sits down and opens it slowly. It contains a piece of paper,
meticulously folded.*

She opens it and reads:

My big little one.

I know you had the strength to wait to open this box. So you
are ready to hear what I have to say.

I am your mother. There has never been any other.

Understand that I am Youmna and you came from my
tummy.

My big little one, are you angry?

I haven't always lied to you. What I said about your mother was often true.

The journey and you came about at the same time. As soon as I felt that you were there, I made a decision.

I thought for me it's done. I can accept that. Not for the child. My child will not go hungry.

It's a girl, I know it.

My daughter will go to school, with her hair dishevelled if she likes.

She'll walk head held high and look straight in front.

She'll think for herself.

She'll choose the first day of her life as a woman.

She will love openly with her face in the wind.

She'll give birth to her children in broad daylight.

And will laugh giving birth to girls.

My big little one, are you angry?

I taught you how to choose on your own what was good for you and to speak only the truth.

And then I lied to you. I decided for you.

My big little one, without this lie, you would never have left, I know.

Here there is nothing for us.

And together we wouldn't have made it.

This has got nothing to do with my ears and everything to do with the laws that prevent men from living here where necessity brings them.

You saw them, didn't you, those that arrive as families and are left at the door?

Those that manage to get in and then live the rest of their lives hiding away?

I didn't want that for us.

I'm writing this letter before you're even born, before discovering the shape of your face, the strength of your scent. A deal I've made with myself so I have no choice.

You'll be a woman when you open it.

I am intensely confident.

Don't be sad any longer, my little fledgling, we are of the same female lineage growing like wild herbs in an unkempt vegetable patch.

My big little one, everything is still possible.

You are the Nour of my life.

Because I am your mother and I carried you.

13.

NOUR

I place the letter next to the piece of paper that allows me to leave and come back.

Nour speaks the words then signs looking at her hands.

I accept.

Youmna is at home. In our tiny little house, on our bit of garden with our tree, our two beds, our four blankets and our four sheets, our two mattresses and our two pillows, our mat, our two saucepans, and our pot, our four plates and three matching glasses, our teapot, our twelve assorted utensils, our two toothbrushes, our brush, our comb, our two towels, our green suitcase, our four complete outfits, our metal dish, our two pairs of shoes, our shelf and our four books.

She is waiting for me.

Blackout.

WWW.OBERONBOOKS.COM

Follow us on Twitter @oberonbooks
& Facebook @OberonBooksLondon